MT SAN JACINTO COLLEGE
SAN JACINTO CAMPUS
1499 N STATE ST
SAN JACINTO, CA 92583

American Waterways:
Canal Days

Edited by Jeanne Munn Bracken

Canals improved transportation and the local economy, as stores sprang up around the canalways. (NY Public Library)

Discovery Enterprises, Ltd.
Carlisle, Massachusetts

All rights reserved. No part of this book may be reproduced, stored in a retrieval system, or transmitted in any form or by any means, electronic, mechanical, photocopied, recorded, or otherwise, without prior written permission of the authors or publisher, except for brief quotes and illustrations used for review purposes.

© Discovery Enterprises, Ltd., Carlisle, MA 1997

ISBN 1-878668-75-7 paperback edition
Library of Congress Catalog Card Number 96-86724

10 9 8 7 6 5 4 3 2 1

Printed in the United States of America

Subject Reference Guide:

Cataloging in Publication Data:

American Waterways: Canal Days Edited by Jeanne Munn Bracken.
 Perspectives on History Series

1 Editor
2 Series

1. Canal-boats   2. Canals — United States — History
3. United States — History — 1783-1865

Dewey 386.46   Library of Congress   HE 395

Acknowledgments:

The editor recognizes the vital contributions of the historians from whose works she has drawn and her reference colleagues throughout the Minuteman Library Network, especially Beverly Shank at the Medford Public Library, the staff at the Wellesley Public Library (Susan Posner in particular), Susan Paju and others at the Acton Memorial Library, the staff of the Reuben Hoar Library in Littleton, and, as always, to her co-workers at the Lincoln Public Library.

Illustrations:

Cover art: Detail of a painting from the Albany Institute of History and Art.
Other illustrations from the National Archives, except where noted in the text.

Table of Contents

The Canal Era in America 7
by Jeanne Munn Bracken
Transportation 7

Colonial and Young America 10
Inland Navigation 10
The Patowmack Canal 11
Canals in the Colonies 13
The Middlesex Canal 14

The 19th Century: Heyday of the Canals 16
The Erie Canal 17
The Pennsylvania Canals - The Portage Railroad 20
The Morris Canal 21
Frances Trollope Comments on the Canals 22
The Wabash and Erie Canal 24

The Canals Today 26
The Songs 29
The E-RI-E 29
Low Bridge! Everybody Down or Fifteen Years on the Erie Canal 30

Who (and What) Made Them Run 32
Building the Canals 32
What Moved the Canals: Mules, and More 34

Working on the Canals 37
On the Wabash and Erie 40
Home on the Canal 42
The Story of Marie Colbert Mose 44
Business was thriving along the canals… 46

Family Life on the Canals 47
Children of the Canallers 50
Life on the canals was dangerous for children… 51
Sickness on the Canals 52

Passengers on the Canals 54
   Nathaniel Hawthorne 54
   Charles Dickens 55

The Canals Endure 59

Suggested Further Reading 60

Dedication

I dedicate *American Waterways: Canal Days* to my mother
Laura P. Losefsky,
because she always believes in me.

ROCHESTER
AND
ALBANY.

Red Bird Line of Packets,
In connection with Rail Road from Niagara Falls to Lockport.

1843.  1843.

12 *hours ahead of the Lake Ontario Route!*

The Cars leave the Falls every day at 2 o'clock, P. M. for Lockport, where passengers will take one of the following new

Packet Boats 100 Feet Long.
THE EMPIRE!
Capt. D. H. Bromley,
THE ROCHESTER
Capt. J. H. Warren,

and arrive in Rochester the next morning at 6 o'clock, and can take the 8 o'clock train of Cars or Packet Boats for Syracuse and Albany, and arrive in Albany the same night.

☞ Passengers by this route will pass through a delightful country, and will have an opportunity of viewing Queenston Heights, Brock's Monument, the Tuscarora Indian Village, the combined Locks at Lockport, 3 hours at Rochester, and pass through the delightful country from Rochester to Utica by daylight.

N. B.---These two new Packets are 100 feet long, and are built on an entire new plan, with

Ladies' & Gentlemen's Saloons,

and with Ventilators in the decks, and for room and accommodations for sleeping they surpass any thing ever put on the Canal.

For Passage apply at Railroad and Packet Office, Niagara Falls.

September, 1843.   T. CLARK, J. J. STATIA, } Agents

Ad for canal trip

The Canal Era in America
by
Jeanne Munn Bracken

By the time Europeans settled in the New World, the notion of canals was an old one. The first known transport canal was dug in China even before the birth of Christ. In the Middle Ages, the Dutch used canals to reclaim lowlands from the sea. In Venice, Germany, England and elsewhere, canals provided transportation routes, a water supply, irrigation, water power, flood control and swamp drainage.

Canals in the United States, not surprisingly, began at the East Coast with the former British colonies and pushed westward into the interior along with the population. These artificial waterways were most important east of the Mississippi River, because the movement of settlers beyond that great interior river coincided with the rise of the railroads, which would be built more cheaply and without regard for the availability of connecting navigable waters.

Transportation

Canals served many purposes. While water transportation was vital in the pre-motorized era, rivers often had shifting sandbars, rapids, currents, waterfalls and such barriers. Canals allowed inland settlers to ship their grain and other crops to market. Sea voyages were shortened by some of the canals and in other instances the distance between cities was significantly shortened.

Benjamin Franklin was one colonial who saw the value of canals.

Source: Letter to S. Rhodes in Philadelphia from London, 1772, in Archer Butler Hulbert's *The Great American Canals* vol. 1,(Cleveland: The Arthur H. Clark Company, 1904), p. 25.

Rivers are ungovernable things, especially in Hilly Countries. Canals are quiet and very manageable. Therefore they are often carried on here by the Sides of Rivers, only on ground above the Reach of Floods, no other Use being made of Rivers than to supply occasionally the waste of water in the Canals. I warmly wish Success to every Attempt for Improvement of our Country.

As time passed and canals were built in more areas of the new country, their importance also grew.

Source: Hulbert, vol. 2, *ibid.*, p. 64-6.

It is calculated that the expense of transporting on a canal, amounts to one cent a ton per mile, or one dollar a ton for one hundred miles, while the usual cost by land conveyance, is one dollar and sixty cents per hundredweight, or thirty-two dollars a ton for the same distance. The certainty of this mode of transportation is evident. A loaded boat can be towed by one or two horses, at the rate of thirty miles a day....A vessel on a canal is independent of winds, tides, and currents, and is not exposed to the delays attending conveyances by land; and with regard to safety, there can be no competition. The injuries to which commodities are exposed when transported by land, and the dangers to which they are liable when conveyed by natural waters, are rarely experienced on canals....(C)anals operate upon the general interests of society, in the same way that machines for saving labor do in manufactures; they enable the farmer, the mechanic, and the merchant to convey their commodities to market...cheaper than by roads...they diminish the distance between places, and therefore encourage the cultivation of the most...remote parts of the country....Canals are advantageous to towns and villages (increasing the markets) open to population, enlarging old and erecting new towns...(increasing wealth) and extending foreign commerce."

While we commonly think of canals as a phenomenon of the Nineteenth Century, which certainly saw the height of their popularity in America, their importance extends both before and after that heyday. Let us look first at the changing impact of the artificial waterways over the centuries of American history, era by era. Then we can examine the people (and animals) who lived and traveled the old canals.

The early colonists saw the advantage of certain canal routes (although the waterways were not necessarily built within their lifetimes). The post-Revolutionary new country began to expand the canals with the movement of settlers towards the interior of the continent. The Industrial Revolution in the early to mid-Nineteenth Century came during the height of the canals and their importance. Over the past century their extent has waned, although some canals are economically vital to this day and others survive in altered states.

From a slow beginning before the War of 1812 to the surge that followed the opening of the Erie Canal in the 1820s, the Canal Era stretched into the next two decades. By the 1840s there were over 3000 miles of canals in the United States, with continuous transportation available from New York Harbor to the Great Lakes, the Ohio Canals to the Ohio River to the Mississippi, to New Orleans and the Gulf of Mexico. At the same time the railroads were growing, often alongside the canals themselves.

Source: Hulbert, Archer Butler, *Pilots of the Republic; the Romance of the Pioneer Promoter in the Middle West* (Chicago: A.C. McClurg & Co., 1906), p. 35-6.

[Transportation was a major factor] in [the] great social movement (to the west), especially the Erie Canal which was...achieved by the patient genius of (DeWitt) Clinton....(the Cumberland Road) was built from the East into the Western wilderness—from a town but little known to an indefinite destination where the towns were hardly yet named. Its promoters were men of faith in the West, hopeful of its prosperity....(T)he same was...true of our first three great canals, the Erie, the Chesapeake and Ohio, and the Pennsylvania. These were not built as avenues of commerce between great Eastern cities, but rather from the East to the awakening West, to the infant hamlets of Buffalo and Pittsburg.

By horseback it took a month to get from Buffalo to New York; by canal less than a week. By railroad, though, the trip was accomplished (in the 1860s) in a day. The canals' importance declined as the mileage of tracks grew; it was cheaper to build railroads than canals, and tracks didn't freeze to the point of uselessness in northern winters. The canals suffered in comparison, but they have left a strong legacy in America, in song and story, and the names that are remembered with them are etched in the country's history: George Washington, DeWitt Clinton, and even the young Jim Garfield, a canalboat driver in the fists-flying, rough-and-tumble era, grew up to be President James Garfield.

Colonial and Young America

Inland Navigation

Source: Hulbert, *ibid.*, pp. 212-213.

Looking back over the colonial history of America it is very interesting to note the part that was played in our country's development by inland navigation. Practically all the commerce of the colonies was moved in canoes, sloops and schooners; the large number of Atlantic seaboard rivers were the roads of the colonies, and there were no other roads. In Pennsylvania and Georgia a few highways were in existence; in the province of New York there were only twelve miles of land carriage. Villages, churches, and courthouses in Maryland and Virginia were almost always placed on the shore of the rivers, for it was only by boat that the people could easily go to meeting or to court. Indeed, the capital of the country, Washington, was located upon the Potomac River, partly for the reason that its founders believed that the Potomac was to be the great commercial highway of the eastern half of the continent.

The Pilgrims landed at Plymouth in 1620 and a mere seven years later proposed digging a canal between the mainland and Cape Cod for defense and to shorten the route south from Boston. That colonial dream only became a 20th century reality in 1914, when Woodrow Wilson was president.

The Patowmack Canal

Many colonial and post-revolutionary leaders recognized the value of canals to improve water transportation and for other purposes. George Washington himself proposed at least two canals. One along the Mohawk Valley in New York to the Great Lakes was opened a quarter of a century after his death—as the Erie Canal. And, in 1774, even before the first shots rang out at Lexington and Concord, he had backed one along the Potomac, past the Great Falls into the interior. Washington headed the company that built the "Patowmack Canal," which some years after his death became part of the Chesapeake and Ohio Canal.

Source: Hulbert, *ibid.*, p. 75.

The plan of the Potomac Company was to improve the navigation of the Potomac to the most advantageous point on its headwaters and build a 20-mile portage road to Dunkard's Bottom on the Cheat River. With the improvement of the Cheat and Monongahela rivers, a waterway, with a 20-mile portage, was secured from the Ohio to tide-water on the Potomac.

Washington's plan, however, didn't stop here. This proposed line of communication was not to stop at the Ohio, but the northern tributaries of that river were to be explored and rendered navigable, and portage roads were to be built between them and the interlocking streams which flowed in to the Great Lakes.

Elkanah Watson, a colonial-era American who studied canals in Holland ("foul-smelling") and elsewhere, is probably best remembered by civil engineers. Watson studied various canal proposals and helped design some of them.

Source: Watson, Elkanah, *Men and Times of the Revolution*; or, *Memoirs of Elkanah Watson, Including his Journals of Travels in Europe and America, from the year 1777 to 1842, and his Correspondence with Public Men, and Reminiscences and Incidents of the American Revolution*, edited by Winslow C. Watson, 2d ed. (New York: D. Appleton & Co., 1861), pp. 281-2.

At (George Washington's) suggestion (*around 1786*), I proceeded up the southern shore of the (Potomac) River, 22 miles from Alexandria, to examine the proposed route of the canal. The extent of this artificial navigation was designed to be about a mile, respectively, at the Seneca, Great, and Little Falls. Eleven miles above Alexandria are the Lower Falls, where the river descends in curling waves 36 feet in a quarter of a mile. Here the contemplated canal will be a mile and a quarter, situated on the north side of the river. We reached, eleven miles further, the Great Falls, which are a stupendous exhibition of hydraulic power. The whole river rushing down amid rocks and impediments, wave pressing upon wave, like the surging of the ocean in a tempest, produced a roaring which we distinctly heard at the distance of a mile. At this place, the entire fall is 75 feet, embracing a vertical descent of 23 feet, which adds infinitely to the imposing scene. Here existed the most serious obstacle to the execution of the (canal)....

"In 1808 I again visited these places. Canals and locks had been completed, round the Little and Great Falls, and also at the Shenandoah and Seneca Falls. Considerable improvements had been made in the bed of the river, above these works. The navigation of the Shenandoah, an important branch of the Potomac, had been opened...but much still remained to be done, to perfect the navigation of the Potomac to Fort Cumberland...."

Canals in the Colonies

The Patowmack Canal, built between 1786 and 1808, used five locks and five bypass canals to make the Potomac navigable. Wheat, corn, rye, flour, whiskey, pig iron, pork, beef, linseed oil, and of course tobacco, moved down river around the falls. In those days immediately after the Revolution, the new states had to discuss "interstate commerce" and navigation issues. The Annapolis Convention in 1786, called partly as a result of Potomac River trade issues, led to the Constitutional Convention in Philadelphia in 1787.

William Penn was another visionary who saw the value in a canal from the Schuylkill to the Susquehenna Rivers, which became a reality early in the next century.

Two of the earliest canals were in the South. The James River and Kanawa Canal ran seven miles from Richmond, Va., around waterfalls to Westham, providing a smooth shipping route for flour, tobacco, various grains, and whiskey; the flatboats were poled by slaves. The Santee and Cooper Canal in South Carolina, begun in 1792 and completed eight years later, ran twenty miles between two rivers, from Charleston into the interior. The area's rice planters had opposed the project, fearing a disruption of their vital water supply, but the cotton planters favored the canal for its improved transportation possibilities. Both industries flourished in the region. This first American canal, with three locks, was built by the labor of slaves from nearby plantations, many of them women.

The Middlesex Canal

In 1793 John Hancock, Governor of Massachusetts, approved the Middlesex Canal between the Merrimack and Medford Rivers and thence to Boston Harbor. Its stone locks were the first project to use hydraulic cement in America.

Source: "Ballou's Pictorial Drawing-Room Companion" vol. X no. 11, September 15, 1855, quoted by Lewis M. Lawrence in *The Middlesex Canal* (Boston: n.p., 1942), p. 123.

Very pleasant was voyaging on the Middlesex Canal in the olden time, in fine weather. Your progress was slow, but it was sure. Three miles an hour was about the maximum. It was a good day's work to go from Boston to Lowell. You embarked at Charlestown in a trimbuilt barge with a very comfortable cabin occupying nearly all the length of the craft inboard, drawn by two horses harnessed tandem. At the very outside you entered a lock. The gates enclosed you in a damp wooden receptacle, and you seemed to be hopelessly lost to society in the bottom of a mouldy chest. But right ahead of you the water came sizzling and streaming down from above, and you gradually found yourself rising in the world, finally coming up to quite a respectable elevation.

The Middlesex Canal in Lowell added to its own demise, by transporting railroad ties for the construction of the Boston and Lowell Railroad, completed in 1835.

Then the gates swung open; the horses were put to, and you resumed your voyage. Slowly moved the laden boat through the still water, between smiling hedge-rows, through patches of woodland, under low bridges, and past pleasant villages....Sometimes the canal widened into a miniature lake....Ever and anon a "sail ahead" would appear in the shape of a vast flatboat, laden with flour or lumber, or the produce of some of the nascent factories, or it may be a huge raft of timber came floating down with two or three mariners in charge, an old spavined horse dragging the establishment along....

Two more canals were important in this era in Massachusetts to improve the navigation of the Connecticut River. The South Hadley Falls Canal was less than two miles long but part of it was bored through solid rock, 40 feet deep and 300 feet long; this canal boasted the first inclined plane in America (a railroad-like system used in lieu of water locks). The Montague Falls Canal was three miles long with eight locks and two dams; it's still in use today.

Not all of the canal building action was taking place along the East Coast, though. The fierce rapids in the Saint Mary's River on the Michigan/Canadian border was first skirted by a Canadian canal in 1799, built by a fur company; it was destroyed by the United States during the War of 1812.

The 19th Century: Heyday of the Canals

The first half of the 19th century saw a great swell in the number of canals in America.

Source: Harlow, Alvin F., *Old Towpaths; the Story of the American Canal Era* (New York and London: D. Appleton and Company, 1926), p. 73.

Between 1820 and 1830 over 800 miles of canals were opened to navigation in New York, Pennsylvania, Delaware, and Maryland—namely the Erie, Champlain, Oswego, Seneca, Delaware and Hudson, Chesapeake and Delaware, Schulykill, Union and some shorter ones. In 1830 full 1300 miles more were well under way and most of it nearing completion.

The Union Canal and the Cumberland and Oxford Canal in Maine (moving timber from the Sebago Lake interior to tidewater Atlantic shores); the Blackstone Canal (proposed from Narragansett Bay in Rhode Island to Worcester in Massachusetts, which ran forty-five miles with a granite lock nearly every mile); The Enfield and Farmington Canals in Connecticut (the latter was supposed to reach the Saint Lawrence River but ended in Northampton, Massachusetts, a mere seventy miles away); The Bellows Falls Canal in Vermont, another "improvement" of the Connecticut; the two and one-half mile long Louisville and Portland Canal in Kentucky, around the falls of the Ohio; New Jersey's Delaware and Raritan Canal, carrying Pennsylvania coal to New York City; the Chesapeake and Delaware Canal, running nineteen miles between the Delaware River and the head of Chesapeake Bay; the expansion of the Patowmack Canal into the Chesapeake and Ohio, stretching from Georgetown on the Potomac past Harper's Ferry toward Pittsburg in central Pennsylvania—were constructed primarily for transportation of goods and passengers. The Dismal Swamp Canal, twenty-two miles from Hampton Roads in Virginia to Albemarle Sound in North Carolina, had a second purpose: to drain the 2200 square mile Great Dismal Swamp. The Pawtucket Canal around the falls in the Merrimack River at Lowell, Massachusetts, also had a dual purpose: to move products, but especially to provide water power for the cotton mills that rose along the river bank.

All of these projects were valuable for their regions, but some carried greater importance or interest.

The Erie Canal

Thoughts of the American Canal Era inevitably bring the Erie Canal to mind. Following the Mohawk Valley westward from New York's Albany area to Erie of the Great Lakes, it was vitally important for many reasons. One of its first economic impacts was providing access to the salt springs at Syracuse; it was unusual in that it was funded by the state rather than by the federal government. As foresighted as Thomas Jefferson had been about canals in other areas, he refused to back the use of federal funds for the Erie Canal.

Source: Harlow, *op. cit.*, p. 46.

[The Erie Canal] is a splendid project and may be executed a century hence....[Y]ou talk of making a canal *three hundred and fifty miles long through a wilderness*! It is little short of madness to think of it at this day.

The Erie project supporters tried to point out the benefit for the whole country, not just for New York, but Jefferson was not interested. Governor DeWitt Clinton, in the face of opposition and abuse, led the state to the completion of "Clinton's Ditch," built over several phases. One decision was to link the Hudson River to Lake Erie rather than to Lake Ontario, which would be of greater benefit to the Canadians. Eventually, feeder canals were built to Lake Ontario and into the Finger Lakes as well as north to Lake Champlain and south into Pennsylvania. Freight rates dropped eighty-five percent upon its completion. The Erie became a principal route for westbound immigrants and eastbound crops and natural resources. The Erie Canal was also ultimately responsible for the development of New York City from an unimportant port to a world leader. While workers on other canals were "canallers," the Erie folk called themselves "canawlers."

Source: Drago, Harry Sinclair, *Canal Days in America* (New York: C. N. Potter, 1972), p. 188.

Much of the folklore of the Erie is woven around the multiplicity of bridges built by the canal commissioners. Eighty were constructed between Little Falls and Schenectady alone. In the vernacular of the day they were referred to as "occupation bridges," that is, they were constructed by the state in fulfillment of a pledge to provide farmers whose lands had been severed by the canal with bridges for cattle crossing and pedestrian traffic. But the economy-minded state did not feel obliged to build them very high. They were so low, in fact, that a person standing on the deck of a canal boat had to stoop in passing beneath one or risk being decapitated. Packet-boat passengers quickly learned to heed the captain's bellowing cry: "Low Bridge! Everybody down!"

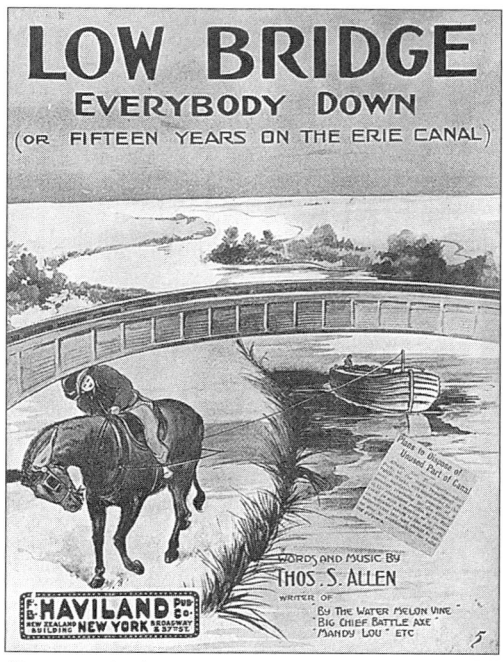

"Low Bridge! Everybody down!" was a phrase that found its way into the canaller's songs.

The famous Lockport "Fives" (or "Combines" as canawlers preferred to call them) are generally regarded as the single most spectacular accomplishment of the Erie engineers.

These pairs of five locks resembled a flight of stairs as they took the canal toward the terminus at Lake Erie. (Courtesy of the New York Public Library)

At its height in 1845, there were 25,000 men, women and children working on 4000 boats on the Erie Canal. Few of the canals survived into the railroad age, but the Erie did.

The Pennsylvania Canals -
The Portage Railroad

Also extremely important were the series of canals built in Pennsylvania, which totaled 1000 miles by 1840. The Schuylkill Navigation Company canalized the Schuylkill river to a major anthracite coal region. The Union Canal, seventy-seven miles long, had over a hundred lift locks, including sixteen in a tunnel west of Lebanon. The Delaware and Hudson ran 107 miles from Honesdale, Pennsylvania, to Kingston, New York on the Hudson, taking coal to New York markets. The Susquehenna Canal, from Pennsylvania into Maryland, ran forty-five miles. The granddaddy of them all, though, was the Pennsylvania Main Line Canal, which ran between Philadelphia and Pittsburg. This engineering wonder was half canal, half railroad, with boats running on train tracks over the crest of the Allegheny Mountains on the Portage Railroad.

On the Pennsylvania system, sectional canal packets rode on the portage railroad before returning to the canal.

Source: Hulbert, *op. cit.*, pp. 250+.

...[C]anal boats could traverse the central portion [of Pennsylvania] as early as 1834, and the uninformed must wonder how a canal-boat could vault the towering crest lying between Hollidaysburg and Johnstown, which the Pennsylvania Railway crosses with difficulty...more than two thousand feet above sea-level. The answer to this introduces us to the Alleghany Portage Railway, a splendid piece of early engineering....The feat was accomplished by means of inclined planes; the idea was not at all new, but, under the circumstances, it was wholly an experiment. The plan was to build a railway which could contain eleven sections with heavy grades, and between them ten inclined planes. A canalboat having been run into a submerged car in the basin on either side of the mountain, it could be drawn over the level by horses or locomotives, and sent over the summit...on the inclines by means of stationary engines. The scheme was first advanced early in the history of the canal, but it was not finally adopted until 1831, and in three years the portage railway was opened for traffic. The ten planes averaged about 2000 feet in length and about 200 feet in elevation...the total length of the road was 36 miles.

The Morris Canal

New Jersey's Morris Canal opened in 1831 between Phillipsburg on the Delaware and Newark, ran 100 miles, carrying freight to New York Harbor.

Source: Drago, *op. cit.*, pp. 119+.

...[T]he directors of the Morris engaged Professor James Renwick of Columbia University, an Englishman, to devise a practical means of getting the canal up and down from Lake Hopatcong, a matter of more than 1600 feet in ninety miles. Since the average lift and fall of a canal lock was six feet, Renwick convinced the director of the company by some simple mathematics that getting through to the Delaware by a system of lockage would require the building of upwards of three hundred locks, the cost of which would run into millions of dollars. Instead he advised a series of inclined planes....In the simplest terms, the inclined plane was nothing more than a short boat-railway up which a canal boat could be raised or lowered by cable (hempen ropes were used in the beginning), an ascending boat counterbalanced by one that was descending. The power was supplied by a stationary engine, or, as in the Morris canal, by water power. Renwick found it necessary to build 23 inclined planes, but only a like number of locks. It was one of the finest engineering feats in canal history.

Source: Rockland, Michael Aaron, *Snowshoeing Through Sewers* (New Brunswick, NJ: Rutgers University Press, 1994), p. 84-5.

Sometimes a trip on an inclined plane was less than smooth. The heavily loaded boat "Electra" was making its maiden trip on the canal in the early 1830s. Just as it started down the inclined plane at Boonton, the chain to which the cradle was affixed snapped. A newspaper told the story:

"Gathering momentum, the boat and its tons of pig iron went hurtling down the plane with the captain's wife and two children aboard. It hit the water just as a toboggan might and splashed water for hundreds of feet. Not only that, but its momentum was so great it skittered along the surface like a modern hydroplane, then lifted its bow at a crazy angle and finally hurdled over an embankment twenty feet high and landed with a crash in some trees. White-faced and trembling bystanders rushed to rescue the captain's wife and family. As the wife emerged uninjured from the cabin they breathlessly explained just how the breaking of the chain had caused the accident. "Why," she said, "it was a mighty fast trip, I'll allow, but I thought that was the way the thing worked."

Frances Trollope Comments on the Canals

Frances Trollope, mother of the writer Anthony, visited America in the 19th century and ruffled some feathers with her frank opinions on the manners of the Americans. Following is her commentary on her canal ride experiences.

Source: Trollope, Frances, *Domestic Manners of the Americans*, edited by Donald Smalley. Gloucester, MA: Peter Smith, 1974, p. 369+.

The first sixteen miles from Albany we travelled in a stage, to avoid a multitude of locks at the entrance of the Erie canal; but at Schenectedy we got on board one of the canal packetboats for Utica. With a delightful party, of one's own choosing, fine temperate weather, and a strong breeze to chase the mosquitos, this mode of travelling might be very agreeable, but I can hardly imagine any motive of convenience powerful enough to induce me again to imprison myself in a canal boat....We reached Utica at twelve o'clock the following day, pretty well fagged by the sun by day, and a crowded cabin by night; lemon-juice and iced-water (without sugar) kept us alive. But for this delightful recipe, feather fans, and eau de Cologne, I think we should have failed altogether; the thermometer stood at 90 [degrees].

Mrs. Trollope also visited the Morris Canal and found something there to admire in Americans after all.

Source: Trollope, *ibid.*, pp. 347-8.

We spent a delightful day in New Jersey, in visiting, with a most agreeable party, the inclined planes, which are used instead of locks on the Morris canal. This is a very interesting work; it is one among a thousand which prove the people of America to be the most enterprising in the world....The expense is less than a third of what locks would be for surmounting the same rise. If we set about any more canals, this may be worth attending to.

This Morris canal is certainly an extraordinary work...at one point [it] runs along the side of a mountain at thirty feet above the tops of the highest buildings in the town of Paterson, below; at another it crosses the falls of the Passaic in a stone aqueduct sixty feet above the water in the river....There is no point in the national character of the Americans which commands so much respect as the boldness and energy with which public works are undertaken and carried through. Nothing stops them if a profitable result can be fairly hoped for. It is this which has made cities spring up amidst the forests with such inconceivable rapidity; and could they once be thoroughly persuaded that any point of the ocean had a hoard of dollars beneath it, I have not the slightest doubt that in about 18 months we should see a snug covered rail-road leading direct to the spot.

The Wabash and Erie Canal

There were many important canals built in the middle west, in Ohio, Indiana, and Illinois. The Wabash and Erie connected Evansville on the Ohio River to the Miami and Ohio Canal, a distance of 187 miles.

The Miami and Erie Canal, crossing the Great Miami River.

Source: "Through Indiana by Stagecoach and Canal Boat: the 1843 Travel Journal of Charles H. Titus," edited by George P. Clark. In *Indiana Magazine of History*, vol. 85 (September 1989), pp. 234-5.

The Wabash and Erie canal affords the greatest facilities of transportation to the farmer and merchant of the Maumee and Wabash vallies (sic)—two of the most fertile regions in the whole world. By means of this canal, the farmer in the upper Wabash—which is the most fertile part of that valley—finds a ready market for all his surplus produce, at a good price....Before this canal was constructed, all the produce was transported by wagons to the river, & thence conveyed in flat boats to a southern market, where, after all the labor & expense of transportation, it generally commanded but a small price. A new day has now dawned upon the agriculturist of this region. Now, with but moderate industry & common prudence, he cannot fail of becoming independent, & even wealthy...

Source: Harlow, *op. cit.*, p. 43.

In the first three or four decades after 1800 the young giant [America] stretched his limbs, discovering something of his power and began to grow. It was during those decades that practically all of our greater canals were built. And it was within the span of those few brief years that the railroads came in turn and dealt the death blow to the canals.

The Canals Today

Many of the first investors in the American canals were Europeans, and much of their money was lost in the financial slump of 1837. Thereafter, they went into railroad finance instead. Those who made the most money on the canals were not the financiers or those who built them, but those who sold things to the canal builders: land, food, tools, clothing and other services.

Source: Harlow, *op. cit.*, pp. 74, 80-82.

The whole land was aflame with the fever of progress. "Freight could now be moved," says the historian McMaster, "from New York to Buffalo through the Erie Canal for four cents a ton per mile, tolls included. These rates revolutionized business...West as well as east became [the merchant's] market....Banks were multiplying. Insurance companies, steamboat, pike and canal companies, mills and factories were springing up on every hand. The whole course of life was changed.

Tens of thousands of men who under the old conditions would have been doomed to eke out a scanty livelihood by farming or by cobbling or by toiling in the crowded ranks of unskilled labor, now found new occupations opening before them. They became mill hands and operatives; they turned machinists and mechanics; they served as engineers and firemen on the steamboats, as clerks and bookkeepers in banks and insurance companies; they handled freight, tended the gates on the turnpike or the bridges on the canals; drove the horses that dragged the canal boats or found employment in some of the older industries, which, such as tailoring and printing...and carpentry, had been greatly expanded....*But right behind the canals came the railroads..." Canals*, said one faction, are facts; railroads are theories, and are opposed to the habits and feelings of our people, for they create monopolies in transportation. A farmer cannot own railroad wagons. But for a hundred dollars he can buy a boat, or with the help of his hands can build one to carry 25 tons. To move such a load by railroad would require eight carriages and a locomotive, costing $4,000. Into his boat the farmer can put an assorted cargo of flour, bacon,...plank, lumber and vegetables, draw it to market with his own horses, sell at any village on the way, and bring it back loaded with what he pleases. Does anybody suppose railroads will take on loads offered anywhere along the line? No, indeed! The farmers must haul them to the stopping places. Canals will carry livestock, hay, firewood, large timber for ship-building, boards and planks. Railroads cannot do this. What would be thought of a load of hay coming along a railroad? The sparks from the locomotive would set it afire before the journey began. Canals are adapted for military purposes; railroads are not. Imagine a regiment of troops with baggage, provisions, ammunition and camp equipage transported by railroad! By canal this can be done and the soldiers live and cook comfortably on the way. The boat will carry tents, food, baggage and ammunition, and may be drawn by the horses or by the men as they walk along the towpath....If locomotives were used it would be necessary to have water-boiling stations every six or seven miles to furnish the engines with tanks of boiling water....In the mountains the cold in winter is often so severe that an axe will break when struck against a tree. Would not rails snap under these conditions as a train passed over them....

But the railroad enthusiasts had some powerful arguments on their side. They pointed out that canals in a northern climate could not be used more than eight months in the year, whereas railroads could be used at least eleven months; and it was even proposed to avoid obstruction by snow in winter and thereby make the railroads available for use the year round by 'building the rails two feet, eight inches above the earth, which, with our great command of wood, can easily be accomplished.' Furthermore, said they, 'it requires a number of years to complete a canal and get it in order, the owners losing the interest of their capital during the time; but a rail-way of considerable length may be completed in a single year.

The canal boosters were wrong about military use of their system and the railroad boosters, while the plan to elevate tracks to avoid snow coverage did not materialize, were right in the long run about tracks being cheaper to lay than canals were to dig, and could stretch across the arid plains without a source of flowing water.

Slowly the railroads surpassed the canals in terms of importance, only to lose much of their power to truck and eventually air freight and travel. Most of the canals were too narrow and shallow for larger barges and the slow speed required to avoid damage to the canal banks was not competitive as the horse-and-buggy era gave way to the space age.

Yet some canals retain their importance today. In the American West, canals provide irrigation for much of the nation's agricultural industry. Portions of the old coastal canals help make up the inland passage from north to south, much used today by pleasure boaters, among others. The Erie Canal and its feeders were enlarged in the early years of the 20th century as the New York State Barge Canal, including electrically-operated locks; again, the drop in commercial traffic has been partly offset by the rise in leisure craft passing through.

Two of the most important canals now showcase cooperation between Canada and the United States. The Soo Canals at the falls in the Saint Mary's River provide passage on both sides of the border for ore and other natural resources from the Great Lakes to Eastern factories and markets. These now form the busiest canal system in the world. To the East, the Saint Lawrence Seaway, built with international cooperation but primarily Canadian financing, provides a channel from the Atlantic to the Great Lakes.

The Mississippi River above Saint Louis required a channel and locks for passage of corn, soybeans and other crops. These and other artificial waterways in Louisiana, Washington state, Florida, Texas and elsewhere still carry a sixth of the nation's freight on barges, saving fuel and labor costs: coal, petroleum products, grain, and minerals.

Some of the other canals are long forgotten, their ditches filling over time, their towpaths overgrown. For many, though, a desire for greater recreational opportunities in a crowded and busy era has given them a second life. Canoes and other small boats lazily drift on these waters, and their towpaths are trails for hikers and bikers. Many have been designated state or national historic parks, well worth a visit to catch a glimpse of the long ago Canal Era in America.

The Songs

Most of the canal songs that survive were based on the Erie, although as time passed and the waterways spread, other canallers devised their own versions of these lyrics.

Source: Low Bridge; Folklore and the Erie Canal, (Syracuse, NY: Syracuse University Press, 1962), pp. 101-105.

The E-RI-E

We were forty miles from Albany,
Forget it I never shall;
What a terrible storm we had that night
On the E-ri-e Canal.

Refrain Oh the E-ri-e was a-rising,
  And the gin was getting low,
  And I scarcely think we'll get a drink
  'Till we get to Buffalo,
  'Till we get to Buffalo.

We were loaded down with barley,
We were chuck up full of rye,
And the captain, he looked down at me
With his goddam wicked eye.

Our captain, he came up on deck,
With a spy glass in his hand,
And the fog, it was so darned thick
That he couldn't spy land.

Two days out from Syracuse
The vessel struck a shoal,
And we like to all been foundered
On a chuck o' Lackawanna coal.

We hollered to the captain
On the towpath, treadin' dirt;
He jumped on board and stopped the leak
With his old red flannel shirt.

Our cook, she was a grand old gal,
She had a ragged dress;
We hoisted her upon the pole
As a signal of distress.

When we got to Syracuse,
The off-mule he was dead,
The nigh mule got blind staggers,
And we cracked him on the head.

The captain he got married
And the cook she went to jail;
And I'm the only son of a gun
That's left to tell the tale.

Low Bridge! Everybody Down or Fifteen Years on the Erie Canal

I've got an old mule and her name is Sal,
Fifteen years on the Erie Canal.
She's a good old worker and a good old pal,
Fifteen years on the Erie Canal.
We've hauled some barges in our day,
Filled with lumber, coal and hay,
And ev'ry inch of the way I know
From Albany to Buffalo.

Chorus: Low bridge, ev'ry body down,
Low bridge, we must be getting near a town
You can always tell your neighbor,
You can always tell your pal,
If he's ever navigated on the Erie Canal.

We'd better look 'round for a job old gal,
Fifteen years on the Erie Canal.
You bet your life I wouldn't part with Sal,
Fifteen years on the Erie Canal.
Giddap there gal we've passed that lock,
We'll make Rome 'fore six o'clock,
So one more trip and then we'll go,
Right straight back to Buffalo.

I don't have to call when I want my Sal,
Fifteen years on the Erie Canal;
She trots from her stall like a good old gal,
Fifteen years on the Erie Canal.
I eat my meals with Sal each day
I eat beef and she eats hay,
She ain't so slow if you want to know,
She put the "Buff" in Buffalo.

Who (and What) Made Them Run

Building The Canals

The construction of the canals is especially remarkable considering the level of engineering and building skills available in the eighteenth and nineteenth centuries. The main tools used on the Erie were picks, shovels and wheelbarrows. Rocks were drilled by hand, loosed with black powder. Horses provided the power for root-cutting plows, earth-moving scoops and stump-pulling. Much of the labor force consisted of Irish immigrants fresh off the boats in New York Harbor.

Source: Drago, *op. cit.*, pp. 173-4.

We never tire of hearing how the Irish bogtrotters built the Erie. Certainly a great number of them — perhaps more than three thousand — put their sweat, blood and muscle into it. As they fought their way through the mosquito — and malaria-infested Montezuma marshes west of Syracuse, toiling in waist-deep muck and water, wearing only a shirt and slouch cap to shield them from the relentless sun, they wrote a page of human endeavor that has seldom been equaled. And for this they were rewarded with the princely wage of $8 a month — or to be more exact, for 28 rainless days of work — and the privilege of sleeping on the floor of a $15-shack along with a dozen others of their kind, their food the cheapest and coarsest the contractor could provide. As a bonus a tot of whisky was doled out to them every two hours — to keep them going.

Several canals built in Ohio in the 1830s to connect various rivers were instrumental in the rise of cities such as Cincinnati, Akron, Columbus and Toledo.

Source: Harlow, *ibid.*, pp. 247-8.

2000 men were at work north of the Licking summit. A village of several dozen shanties was erected for their own use by Irish laborers near the falls of the Cuyahoga; this was the beginning of the present city of Akron. In the following season 3000 teams of horses were at work on that portion of the canal. While a considerable number of Irish laborers had come from the Erie and some Germans from Pennsylvania, the greater part of those who dug the first Ohio Canals were Anglo-Saxon countrymen, mostly farmers' sons, from the vicinity. They earned from $6 to $10 per month....To many of these boys, it was the first opportunity of their lives to earn real money. The work was carried on as nearly as possible the year round. Their pay stopped in bad weather, and it might take all winter to make two months' salary, but the job was regarded as being worth while even at that. Some of them worked on the canal only in their own neighborhood and boarded at home, so that they were able to utilize the bad weather by husking corn and doing other indoor work on their own farms.

The men not at home were lodged in rough shanties, and for some time received a regular allowance of whisky as a part of their rations. Some wriers assert that the allowance was a 'jigger' — a small cup containing not more than a gill (1/2 cup) — per day; but there seems to be good evidence that in some districts they received no less than four per day — at sunrise, at ten o'clock, at noon and before supper. To say nothing of the evil effects of the liquor, this consumed a great deal of valuable time....[T]wo leading commissioners finally put a stop to the practice, causing considerable grumbling but a generally higher efficiency.

Not only did these men dig the canal ditches, but they also blasted tunnels, erected bridges over the canals, and built aqueducts. These aqueducts, engineering feats known at least since Roman times, were bridges with a difference: they carried the canal bed, the water, and the boats across inconvenient streams and rivers in their path. As time passed and the earlier canals proved their value, more construction projects were begun. Working conditions hadn't gotten much better. In 1853, some 2000 men drilled on the Soo Canals project through the northern winter. Living in flimsy housing, stricken by a cholera epidemic, hundreds didn't live to see its completion.

What Moved the Canals: Mules, and More

A variety of power sources were tried out to move the barges and boats on the canals. Steamships, ironically, moved too fast, their wake causing damage to the canal banks. Humans poling the boats, which worked on the early projects over fairly short periods of time, were not satisfactory for the long hauls. Animal power from oxen to horses was also tested and proved satisfactory now and then. But the animal that proved most successful, especially on the Erie Canal, was the mule. Alternately cursed and beloved, the canal mule is remembered in song and legend to this day.

Source: Harlow, *op. cit.*, p. 321.

Somebody was always trying to cipher out a way to get rid of the canal mule. They even gave oxen a severe test on the Middlesex. An ox can pull more than any other draft animal save an elephant. One yoke of oxen drew on the Middlesex a raft of timber calculated to weight 800 tons. But oxen are also the slowest of four-footed animals, their rate of progress being no more than one mile per hour (*3-4 mph was best on the canals*). At that rate of speed the experts decided that 'steers' wouldn't pay.

Source: "Erie Canal" by Joel Swerdlow and Bob Sacha in *National Geographic*, vol. 178 #5 (November 1990), p. 42.

"Mules require less rest, eat rougher food, and are smarter [than horses]. A mule won't walk off a bridge; a horse will."

Source: Garrity, Richard G., *Canal Boatman; my life on upstate waterways* (Syracuse, NY: Syracuse University Press, 1977), p. 22. Reprinted with permission.

[An] incident that happened on one trip concerned an old and clumsy mule. While coming ashore at changing time, the mule stumbled on the horse bridge and fell into the canal. He went completely under the water and did not come up right away. The crew says, 'To heck with him. We won't be bothered by that knothead anymore.' Suddenly the animal came to the surface, climbed up the sloping canal bank, walked along the towpath, took his own place in the team, and stood there waiting to be hitched up to the towline. After a few seasons the canal mules would get on and off the boat at changing time by themselves. They knew their place in the bowstable and on the towpath.

I have been asked many times why mules were used on the canal instead of horses. I knew that canal men considered the mules smarter in many ways. They were also more nimble and surer-footed, climbing in and out of bow stables and up and down horse bridges, were less skittish, and not so apt to be alarmed over unusual sights or sounds along the towpath. Canal animals drank from a bucket of water dipped up from the canal. A horse might drink water contaminated by sewage and become sick, but a mule would refuse it no matter how thirsty it might be.

Another factor was that the hindmost part of a horse sways when it walks or climbs. This sometimes caused it to stumble or miss its footing while getting on or off canal boats.

A horse exiting the bow stable on a horse-drawn canal boat.

As Garrity notes, on the Erie the mules usually belonged to the boat owner, two teams — so one could tow while the other rested. Stables right on the canal boats were their homes, and they rode along with the cargo or passengers when they weren't "on duty." On some canals, a change of animals took place much like the stagecoaches: at certain points along the canal, stables provided a change of mules, the tired animals resting while a new team continued the tow. The mules were also boarded at farms near the canal during the northern winters when the canals were frozen and useless. The mules were, not surprisingly, very important to the success of the operation.

Source: Garrity, *op. cit.*, pp. 9-10.

A canal boat owner was occasionally subjected to costly repair bills for damages to the boats caused by striking objects in the canal or by having the cabins torn off by hitting low bridges when the boats were light. He could also suffer the loss of his mules such as my father did in the RockCut above Lockport.

Once, with our two boats loaded with lumber for Albany, we had left Tonawanda before dark on a summer evening. So when I went to bed I thought we would be below Lockport and on our way over the upper long level when I got up for breakfast. When mother called me the next morning, I was surprised to find out that we were still above the Lockport locks. She did not seem to be her usual cheerful self, and I sensed that something had gone wrong. On inquiring, I was told that our team of mules had fallen into the canal and had drowned a mile or so above the locks. The current had carried the boats along and we were lying tied up at the head of the locks. Nearby, I could see the two drowned mules floating in the canal with their collars and harnesses still on. The current had also carried them down to the locks during the night. The driver was safe, but I could sense the general air of gloom that was felt by everyone on the boats.

When I asked how it happened, I was told that the wind had picked up during the night, and a sudden gust had blown a piece of paper along the towpath toward the mules. This caused the inside mule to shy and crowd the other mule off the towpath into the canal. As they were hitched together, one mule had pulled the other into the canal with him. The towpath in the Rock Cut at this point was six or seven feet above the water's edge, and the night being very dark, the mules soon became entangled in their harnesses and drowned. Had it been daylight they might have been saved.

Working on the Canals

Workers on the eighteenth century Patowmack Canal were hard to find; wages including nearly a pint of rum a day sweetened the deal, but still indentured servants ran away from the canal work. (When they were caught and returned to their labors, their heads and eyebrows were shaved for punishment). Eventually, slaves were rented from nearby plantations to complete the work.

Freight boats, both company fleets and privately-owned, towed barges or boats at one and one-half miles an hour or so. The deluxe packet (passenger) boats moved night and day, promising faster voyages and commanding higher fares. Line (freight) boats and regular passenger boats tied up at night on some of the canals. The soul of the canals were the owner-operators, who lived on their boats, often with their families aboard.

Source: Garrity, *ibid.*, p. 9.

The average individual boat owner at that time had two boats. These were usually bought with a down payment and a mortgage on the boats for the balance of the payment, which was paid out of the boat's earnings. He also had to have six head of stock (mules or horses), collars, harnesses...and other necessary trappings. Hiring competent and reliable drivers and steersmen was another of his problems. He also had to arrange with brokers for cargoes and cargo insurance.

The boat owner's credit had to be good with drydock owners and canal boat suppliers. At the end of the season, he arranged for the boarding of the mules with a nearby farmer. During the winter months, the boats had to be kept pumped out and the boat's equipment looked after, so that it was not stolen before spring came around.

A source of good, dependable labor was not always at hand.

Source: Way, Peter, "Evil humors and ardent spirits: the rough culture of canal construction laborers." *Journal of American History*, vol. 79 #4 (March 1993), pp. 1398, 1425+.

[T]he canallers were not native-born skilled workers with an important social, economic, and political position within American society; they were refugees...who lacked a solid community structure in this new land and whose only resource was their brutal labor power....[The] public presence of these people was generally rough hewn....The message was not one of harmony with employers or even among themselves....Feeling their exclusion from society, canallers reinforced the barrier by assaulting it....At work, in their shanties, and particularly while drinking, they created a distinctive life-style that set them apart from most of society...competing, drinking, brawling, and social rivalries....

Source: Garrity, *op. cit.*, p. 21.

There were...canal drivers who were mature men. Some came from farms; others had driven teams before hiring out to the canal. They were used to animals and knew how to manage them. This was their only responsibility, and they sought no other. In some cases when the boat owner or operator had a boy old enough to drive a team, he would be pressed into service as a driver. The boy had to be clothed and fed anyway, and it saved the board and wages of a man.

While passing through the canal, drivers worked twelve hours each day, six hours on and six hours off. Changing teams and meal times were 7 a.m., 1 p.m., 7 p.m. and 1 a.m., at which time a midnight lunch was set out for each member of the crew in the after cabin. This was standard schedule on canal fleets. I believe it was kept so that the cook did not have to rise too early.

The driver was awakened one hour before changing time to water, feed, and harness the team. While the animals were feeding, the driver washed up; then he and one steersman went back to the after cabin and ate together. As soon as they came back on deck, the steersman on duty called to the driver on the towpath to look for a tie-up post. At times a tree or telegraph pole was used for this purpose. As soon as the boats were stopped, the mules were unhitched from the towline and the horse or change bridge was run out from the boats to the canal bank.

The fresh mules were run ashore, then the tired mules were guided aboard the boat, and the horsebridge was pulled aboard. By that time the fresh team had been hitched to the towline. The tie-up lines were let go and the boats were underway again within fifteen minutes or so. Everything went like clockwork at changing times. The steersman and the driver who had just been relieved washed up, then went back to the after cabin and ate. When the meal was finished, the driver returned to the bowstable, where he watered and fed the team and then removed their harnesses while they were eating. He then cleaned the stable floor, by sweeping the manure and soiled bedding material into a pile and, with the help of a scoop shovel, threw it from the stable into the canal. [The same canal from which washing and drinking water was sometimes drawn!] He then spread about one inch of bedding material over the floor (shavings or sawdust) to help soak up any animal urine. When he had finished taking care of the team he rested until it was time to get them ready for the next six-hour shift or trick on the towpath.

If no tie-up post or tree was convenient, it was possible to make the team changes while the boat was moving, but that was risky, especially at night or when the water had a current.

On the Wabash and Erie

Source: Clark, George P., ed, "Through Indiana by Stagecoach and Canal Boat; the 1843 Travel Journal of Charles H. Titus," *The Indiana Magazine of History*, vol. 85 (September 1989), pp. 219+.

After spending an uncomfortable night in a berth on a canalboat, Titus awakened to discover that the boat was not moving.

We were making no progress. I learned upon inquiry that we had been in that fix since two o'clock and were likely to remain so for three or four hours more...the cause of our delay was, that the gates in the lock where we were, had been opened in the night and permitted to remain so, while those in the lock above remained closed. The consequences of this mismanagement were, that the water was drawn off of the level above us, between the two locks, and it was impossible for us to proceed until the water could be let in at the upper lock and fill the level again. A boy had been sent up to open the gates of the lock above, and the water was already rising. In about two hours the boat floated again, but we proceeded very slowly; the boat rubbing against the bottom every few rods, and sometimes stopping entirely, where we were forced to remain until the rising water floated us off.....*[His trip didn't get any smoother as time went on.]* About four o'clock in the morning we were all aroused by a tremendous racket on, and about the boat, and we all, simultaneously, jumped from our berths and rushed up on deck, to learn what all the outcry could mean. The cry 'The horses are in the canal' made known the cause of the uproar, and on looking ahead we saw that, sure enough, one of the horses and the driver were in the water—which at this point is very deep & the current swift—and both swimming toward the shore for dear life. They soon got out, without any serious injury, & the driver getting on a dry suit of clothes, we went on as usual....The distance from the bridge to the water was, at least, ten feet; but as the water was very deep, neither horse, [n]or driver, experienced any other injury than a good wetting....Friday night, about sunset, commenced raining, and rained powerfully all night. The water in the canal was very low, & the canal narrow; and as it was exceedingly dark, and the hands rather green, they found it difficult to prevent the boat from running against the banks. The pattering of the rain upon the deck, and the clatter and confusion among the men, kept us awake till nearly midnight, and the little sleep I did get, towards morning, was not refreshing. Yet my situation was so much more comfortable than that of the men who worked the boat amid the storm and darkness, that I was kept from murmuring, or finding fault with my position.

Source: Drago, *op. cit.*, p. 285.

By 1850 more than a thousand youths [*ages 12-17*] were walking or riding the towpath [*as drivers. These "hoggees"*] sprang from many different backgrounds—farms, city slums, country villages, and no few were the sons of the Irish bogtrotters who had dug the Erie. After a year on the canal most of them were hard and tough, masters of profanity, and, where custom permitted, could stand up to a bar and down their whisky as neat as any man.

They were on the towpath every day, no matter what the weather. They had to be expert in dropping or raising towlines to permit the passage of fast packets and freighters. If there was a foul-up, the captain vented his wrath on them, which often meant a whipping and/or the withholding of their pay. The standard wage for hoggees ranged from $8 to $10 a month for a season of seven months, payable when the boat tied up for the winter. It was an arrangement that worked in the captain's favor, for a boy could not jump ship without risking loss of the wages he had coming.

Source: Garrity, *op. cit.*, p. 28.

Although the average driver was something of a rascal, all those employed by my father were respectful to Mother and they liked children. The driver's soothing voice and firm hands on the reins kept the team pulling steadily through heavy rain, thunder and lightening storms. He calmed the mules frightened by dogs snapping at their heels or snakes slithering across the towpath.

Canal drivers seldom if ever talked of their home towns or their family backgrounds. They never seemed to plan for the future and were content with a day-to-day existence....They were frequently broke and hungry and often begged drinks and food from canal men they knew until they hired out again....They were a footloose breed of men, all gone now along with the old towpath.

Home on the Canal

An excerpt from the story of former canaller Lester Mose Sr. of the Chesapeake and Ohio.

Source: Elizabeth Kytle, *Home on the Canal* (Cabin John, MD: Seven Locks Press, 1983), p. 173.

...I had [the same feeling] all my life. I did. The whole time I was on the canal. It was lonely. To me, it was lonely. [*This was after the canals' importance shrank considerably in the early years of this century.*] You'd go for eight or nine miles and see nobody. Only thing you'd ever run into would be a locktender, and you wasn't there but a few minutes. But I always did like the mules. One was named Dick; one was named Aleck; one named Matt; and one named Rose.

I took a lot of interest in the mules. Mules was always used. Horses wouldn't stand the travel. There were a few horses along the canal, but not too many and they never stayed long. A mule could stand [canal work] better; they had smaller feet; they were tougher. Horses made an awful good team, but they didn't last long....

Getting a loaded boat started was a hard problem. That's one thing about a team of mules. You start your loaded boat out of the lock, and it's *dead weight*. If you had a good team, they'd just go up against that towline and stretch that line up so-far, and then they'd just stay there a little bit and lay their weight there until the boat started moving so they could make a step. Then they'd made another step. After they went about 25 feet [that way] they didn't have the boat under good headway, but they had the boat moving.

If you got a new team and had mules that was never used to the canal [they] had a little trouble learning to do that. They'd jump around. If you'd talk to them and quiet them down, it didn't take them too long. It might take a couple of weeks or a couple of trips, but they'd come to it.

Source: Harlow, *op. cit.*, pp. 338-9.

Let nothing...cause the impression to get abroad that there were not many worthy men among the canallers—sometimes a bit rough coated, perhaps, but decent and orderly citizens. Among them were those whose freight boats were the floating homes of their captain-owners. Some captains' families remained at home, usually in a village along the line of the canal, where they were apt to tend a thriving truck patch (vegetables) or perhaps even run a little store. Other families spent some seasons aboard the husband's vessel and some ashore. In the heyday of the canals, a village man was sometimes able to rent a boat for a season, upon which he would close up his little home on shore and he and his family would take to the water.

The incredibly small cabin at the stern was usually as neat as a new pin if a woman was on board. There would be colored geranium growing in a tin can on the sill. On some canals, such as the Lehigh, Morris and Delaware Division, where the boats were narrow and the cargo space almost crowded the cabin space out of existence, the cooking was usually done on a stove standing on the open deck....

On the three canals mentioned, the crew not infrequently consisted of two men only, each of whom took turns at driving while the other steered. The man who was steering meantime did the cooking. He would lift the potlid and take a look at the beans, run about forty feet to the stern and give the rudder a twist, trot forward to the stove, put on the coffee and break an egg into it, run back and give the tiller another swing, possibly take out the tiller handle until a bridge was passed, put it in place again and dash forward to snatch off the coffee pot, which was boiling over. When he had gulped down his hasty meal, he would leap to the towpath and drive while the other man ate. One old-timer tells us that if it rained, an umbrella must be held over the stove, but how the steersman could do this under the circumstances described it is hard to guess.

While waiting their turns at loading or unloading points or awaiting repairs on a broken lock or towpath, sometimes fifty or a hundred boats might collect and lie together for days or weeks, while their crews fraternized, and occasionally fought. Fishing, wrestling, foot racing, excursions into the neighboring city or country, card playing, smoking and swapping yarns filled most of these days of waiting for the men, while women sewed, visited and traded gossip and household lore. Old Pennsylvania boatmen laugh yet over the story of Mrs. Captain Jenkins, who was visiting Mrs. Captain Jones while their boats lay in a large fleet in New York Harbor...was so absorbed in conversation with her crony that she paid no attention when a tug picked up the Jones boat's towline and started with it toward the Raritan, unintentionally removing her from the bosom of her family for nearly a week.

Another source reports she was away for a full month. Given how hard these women worked, though, one has to wonder if missing the boat was such an accident!

The Story of Marie Colbert Mose

Source: Kytle, *op. cit.*, pp. 190-1.

There was two of us girls mostly all the time with our father....When one sister was on the towpath, the other was cooking or doing other housekeeping chores....

Women doing laundry on the deck of a canal boat.

We would have our cabins to scrub. Every morning. Make our bunks up. Every morning. We would scrub our boats off *every morning*. From one end to the other. All the decks were scrubbed. Everything. The cabin floors, little staterooms. There was a hole bored in the floor, in the boat, and the water that you scrubbed the floor with would drain down there. Drain right down on the coal. It wasn't that much to hurt anything.

We ate most everything and anything just the same as at home because we carried *plenty of grub*. We could keep food back under the stern of the boat; and the food, it kept good. It was always cool under there; the boat down in the water kept it cool....

We had a little half range. It doesn't have a back to it and it's not nearly as big as a big range. There was a place built for this little stove to be set back in. We cooked everything. Everything. You know, bean sup was a boatsman's great meal. Bean soup and [noodles] made with eggs. Fried chicken. Fish. Coffee. Anything at all. If we wanted to bake, we had our little baker—a regular oven.

The stove burned coal. Because, see, we could use coal off the boat. If you wanted to cook something quick, you used corn cobs. We had a lot. We fed the mules corn, and we'd save the corn cobs. If you had something that didn't take a whole lot of cooking and it was hot, we'd just use the corn cobs, because that would soon die out; the coal would last.

We heated water on the stove, and of course we had our dishpan and our soap dish. We set the dishpan on the table and washed up our dishes. We used Octagon soap. And we'd redd up our table. Leavings from the table went out in the canal.

Source: Waggoner, *op. cit.*, pp. 142-3.

The problems of all canallers were numerous and difficult, partly because the entire enterprise was too new to have been worked out carefully, partly because of the crowded conditions everywhere. The packets and lineboats carried too many passengers. The freighters were too heavily loaded—jammed...with boots, shoes, rope, furniture, stoves, millstones, and farm machinery on their way west, and with fruit, vegetables, meat, cordwood, ashes for the soap factories, and unbelievable quantities of whiskey when they headed back east. The whiskey caused a lot of trouble, because it was cheap and could turn the laborers into a hard-drinking, hard-swearing, hard-fighting lot....The [fighting] admittedly produced one of the greatest of all (canal) problems, becoming so common that it soon was a rare thing to happen upon any canal section where there was not a fist fight in sight. Even the captains were guilty, fighting for emigrant trade to the point of snatching passengers from each other's boats, a practice which was naturally a trouble breeder. In fact, the strip of canal between Albany and Schenectady where most westbound movers embarked soon came to be known as Battleground, for there the skirmishing continued day and night with no holds barred. As a result of this state of affairs passengers could virtually name their own rates, while freight costs dropped form $32 to $1 per ton...there was an element of truth in the saying that 'a well-hardened fist is both judge and jury on the Big Ditch,' for certainly it was usually the bully who [was allowed to pass through locks] first, rules or no rules....In fact, so important to the running of the Big Ditch was the successful fighter, that soon many of the big companies were frankly listing this talent as their top requirement when hiring help.

Business was thriving along the canals...

As the canals threaded their way through the wilderness, towns and cities sprang up to serve the workers.

Source: Garrity, *op. cit.*, pp. 33-4.

Canalside stores stocked anything a canal fleet needed in the way of patent medicines, cooking pots, tinware, candy, food, shoes, clothing, rain gear, and dry goods. Also available were supplies such as hay, oats, straw or shavings, harnesses, horse collars...towlines, and...hardware. It was also possible to take on drinking and cooking water at these places. Kerosene or coal oil had to be obtained at these supply points, as oil lamps were the only type of illumination to be had on canal boats at that time.

Family Life on the Canals

Life for the families of captains and owners who worked on the canals was difficult, with cramped quarters and plenty of work for the older children and the women along with the men. The younger children were especially in peril, and few received as good an education as they might have had the family stayed year-round in a village or city. One of the best reminiscences of life on the Erie Canal comes from Richard Garrity, who spent part of his boyhood in the World War I era with his family on a canal boat.

Source: Garrity, *op. cit.*, pp. 33-34, 11-14, 46.

A captain who had his family on the boats lived a fairly comfortable life, as the woman had the meals on time, did the washing and ironing, kept the cabin clean, and made the beds. She also saw that her husband had a bath occasionally so that he did not get lousy as many other bathless canallers did.

During the canning season many canalmen's wives purchased fruit and vegetables at locks or canalside stores or from farmers along the canal. The boater's wife canned and preserved things in the cabin of the boat, and when the boat was laid up in the fall, the canned goods were taken home for winter use. On the final trip in the fall many families purchased two or three barrels of different kinds of apples, ten or twenty bushels of potatoes, a supply of cabbage and quantities of beets, turnips, squash and other vegetables. These they stored in their earthen-floored cellars and used during the winter.

The first day after starting up or down the canal, fresh meat was usually on the menu. After that, the ice was gone. Then, smoked and salted meats were the general fare until the boats stopped at a canalside grocery store, where the ice and the depleted larder were again replenished. There were many such stores at intervals along the canal....

Home-made bread, pies, cookies, roasts, etc., were baked in the oven of the black iron cook stove in the cabin. Fuel for cooking or heating was never a problem on lumber boats because the boatman sawed up what lumber was needed for firewood from the cargo....

The canal season of 1914 was the last that Mother and all the family were to be on the boats with Father during the canal season. There were then seven children living with Mother and Father in the small living space of a canal boat cabin, the youngest a babe in arms, the next a toddler. The older children missed many days of school during the canal season. There was also the worry of accidents or the drowning of one of the children....It is hard for me to realize how my mother coped with raising her family on a canal boat as long as she did....In 1914...she cooked for the steersman, Father, herself, and seven children. The table had to be set and cleared off twice; there was not room enough for everyone to eat at the same time. The dishes were washed in a dishpan on the cleared-off table. The water for laundering the clothes had to be dipped up from the canal and heated on the woodburning stove in a copper wash boiler. The laundry was done by hand, by rubbing the clothes on a washboard in a galvanized tin tub. When ironing, she heated the old-fashioned irons on top of the wood stove. A clothes line, stretched on posts between the bowstable and the boat's stern cabin, served to dry the clothes. The water to bathe the children had to be heated on the stove. The water for drinking and cooking was dippered into a pail from the barrel on deck and carried into the cabin.

There were no built-in bathroom facilities on a canal boat in those days. You washed your hands and face in a tin wash basin or a bucket of water dipped up from the canal. For the women and small children, the toilet was a slop jar containing a small amount of water, kept out of sight in the stateroom. The men and older boys used the bowstable for privacy....All waste was disposed of by heaving it overboard. No one was shocked by this practice. There was no alternative, and heaving overboard was the answer to all disposal problems from the time the canal opened. There was enough clean water coming in from the feeders and runoff from the fields to cause enough current in the canal to take care of this biodegradable material. Some canallers fashioned a wooden toilet seat which fitted on top of the open bucket for more comfort; others just sat on the rim....

Raising a family in the small space of a canal boat always kept Mother busy keeping all of us children in line and watching constantly that no one fell overboard. Sometimes to get a toddler out from underfoot and into the fresh air, she would tie the child on top of the cabin with a short piece of clothesline, so that it could move but could not fall off the cabin or into the canal. This could only be done when the boats were loaded. Nothing could be on the cabin when the boats were light or empty because of the low bridges. If the boats were traveling light, the small children could be put in the empty cargo hold or midship to play. Here they stayed until Mother was ready to have them back in the cabin. She coped with childhood sicknesses, minor injuries, and took small or large emergencies in stride....

The cabin was furnished with the barest essentials. If there were small children, it had a rocking chair and a kitchen table, usually covered with oilcloth, and four or five stools that were stored under the table when not in use. The meals were prepared on a black wood- and coal-burning cookstove. The floor was either painted or covered with linoleum, and curtains were hung at the windows. Illumination was provided by a kerosene lamp in a bracket on the wall over the table. There was no fly screening on the windows or on the cabin door and hatch. At mealtime Mother used to shoo the flies out of the cabin with a fly chaser. The...sleeping quarters (were)...always called the stateroom. This room—about 15' wide by 6 1/2' long—took up the full inside width of the boat. The floor was about two feet lower than the cabin floor. To enter it, we had to go through a 4-foot-high opening and step down two or three steps. Little or no sunshine ever entered the stateroom; it was always very dim or dark and somewhat damp and musty. The darkness provided some advantage, because when we wished to sleep in the daytime, the flies had a hard time finding the sleeper.

Children of the Canallers

By the early years of the twentieth century, the conditions of canalboat families had caught the attention of the federal government. Social workers became concerned about missed schooling, lack of medical care, child labor, and similar problems.

Source: Springer, Ethel M., "Canal-boat Children," in *Monthly Labor Review*, vol. 16 #2 (February 1923), pp. 3+.

The operation of canal boats is an occupation handed down from father to son. Said one mother: "The children are brought up on the boat and don't know nothin' else, and that is the only reason they take up 'boating.' Boys work for their fathers until they are big enough to get a boat of their own, and it's always easy to get a boat."...

One captain, who had begun boating with his father when he was 5 years of age, said that altogether he had gone to school only 29 months. He seemed to regret his own lack of education and said that when his little girl was old enough to go to school he should stop boating. ...Although the captains usually do some of the driving, especially if the boat travels at night, they consider it a child's job during the day. In dry weather the towpath, which is level except at the approach to the locks, is well beaten down and easy to walk on, but in summer the work is wearisome and hot. In wet weather the path is muddy and slippery, and consequently shoes and clothing get very hard wear. One captain considered himself the best father on the canal, because he provided his boys with rubber boots....

Hours of travel on the canal were practically continuous. Fifteen hours a day was the minimum reported by any of the boat families; 18 was the number of hours most frequently reported; and several families stated they worked longer.... "It never rains, snows, or blows for a boatman, and a boatman never has no Sundays," explained one father. "We dont know it's Sunday," said another, "till we see some folks along the way, dressed up and a-goin' to Sunday school." One captain and his wife who reported working 15 hours a day employed no crew but depended on the assistance of two children, a girl 14 years of age and a boy of 5. The girl did almost all the driving, usually riding muleback, and the parents steered. The little boy helped with the driving, but did not drive for more than a mile or two at a time. The boat was kept moving until the girl could drive no longer, then the boat was tied up for the night. "We'd boat longer hours if the driver felt like it," said the father....

One of the boating households consisted of four persons—the captain and his assistant "deck hand," the captain's wife, and their 11-year-old daughter. The child had been driving, steering and doing housework about the boat for "several years," but she did not like boating and got very lonely. Her father said that she could do anything the "hand" could do, but he felt it necessary to hire a man because, as he put it, "you have to rest once in a while...The women and children are as good as the men," he said. "If it weren't for the children the canal wouldn't run a day." The girl's school attendance for the year 1920-21 had been 89 days out of 177....

Life on the canals was dangerous for children...

Source: Garrity, *op. cit.*, p. 123.

The boats were in Tonawanda, New York, near their house, getting ready for winter, when the following occurred.

While...the second boat [was being pulled] against the current under the Seymour Street bridge, (the author's 5-year-old brother] Charles and my younger sister Gladys were sitting on top of the cabin, where my mother had placed them, with strict instructions not to get down, never dreaming of what would happen.

Suddenly, with Mother busy in the cabin, my small sister excitedly called down, "Mommy, Mommy, Charles is hanging on the bridge!" By the time Mother realized what had happened and rushed up out of the cabin, the boats had moved a considerable distance, and Charles was left hanging to the underside of the bridge over open water. Father was quickly told of his young son's plight. Stopping the slowly moving boat as soon as he could, he started moving back under the bridge, never thinking he would make it before Charles would have to let go. In the meantime, a considerable crowd had collected along the towpath, many of them shouting encouragement to the young lad to hold on just a little longer. An acquaintance of ours had his coat and shoes off, ready to dive in if the boy should let go. But Charles surprised everyone: he hung on until the boat was moved back under him and willing arms lifted him back on the boat. A sigh of relief came from the people on the towpath and many shouted congratulations because he had hung on so long. He must have hung on that bridge for ten minutes!

The author admits that Charles might have gotten the idea from his older brothers, who occasionally grabbed a bridge as the front of a boat pulled under it, then dropped back as the stern passed. Some children did, of course, fall overboard and drown in the canals.

Sickness on the Canals

Sickness, too, was no stranger to the crowded cabins.

Source: Springer, *op. cit.,* pp. 9-11, 19-20.

Very little use of the services of doctors had been made by the canal-boat families. A large proportion of them did not regard ordinary illness as an excuse for sending for a physician. "We never need a doctor," said one father. "We just stay sick until we get well." ...Numerous accidents had occurred among the boat children. Forty-five children had fallen into the canal more or less frequently; 11 had been kicked by mules; 1 had been burned; 1 cut with an axe; another dragged by a mule over a lock gate. One mother said that her four children had had many accidents. The oldest had had his nose broken by a kick from a mule....With the exception of the baby all had fallen into the canal many times, and once when the lock master, by closing the gates too soon, dragged the awning off the deck and the children with it, they were caught between the gate and the boat. In telling about these accidents, the mother seemed to consider them an inevitable part of boating....

Decks of canal boats make a picturesque but somewhat restricted playground. ...The children... who attempt to play ball or hide-and-seek on the narrow decks run great hazards. ...One mother had lost four children while on canal boats. The oldest child had died of "sunstroke"; the second, 5 years of age, had been drowned; another had been burned to death by an explosion of oil on the barge; another, a baby, had died of spinal meningitis after being dropped on the deck of the boat and injured. One of the surviving children had been injured by the oil explosion which killed the third child.

Opportunities for recreation were very meager. Several families, when asked about their pleasures and recreation, replied that they had none. Nearly all said that their only friends were the other boating families. Some complained that the children got lonely and restless. One father who was musical was teaching his children to sing and to play on the banjo and the mandolin. Some of the children spoke of good times swimming in the canal, especially when they reached the lower levels, or were detained for a number of days at the terminal. Unfortunately at this point the water of the canal was much polluted; the towpath, which furnished almost the only playground for the children, was littered with manure and refuse, and children were obliged to find play spaces between the mules standing along the path.

Passengers on the Canals

Quite a few published recollections exist of riding on the canals in packet boats. Charles Dickens, Nathaniel Hawthorne, the Frenchwoman Harriet Martineau, Harriet Beecher Stow, and others, wrote remarkably similar reminiscences despite having experiences on different canals. They wrote of rain that forced passengers to crowd into tiny cabins; they wrote of a lack of privacy; they wrote of monotonous meals; they wrote of poor hygienic habits among their fellow travelers (spitting, for one thing); they all wrote of the tiny, uncomfortable bunks, which Dickens likened to book shelves and insisted weren't much larger. Ladies and children were separated from the men, but only by a curtain. Nathaniel Hawthorne rode on the Erie Canal.

Nathaniel Hawthorne

Source: "The Canal-Boat" in *Mosses from an Old Manse (Tales and Sketches)*. Library of America, New York: 1972, 1974, pp. 345+.

In my imagination, De Witt Clinton was an enchanter, who had waved his magic wand from the Hudson to Lake Erie, and united them by a watery highway....I embarked about thirty miles below Utica....

Behold us, then, fairly afloat, with three horses harnessed to our vessel...in our adventurous navigation of a interminable mud-puddle, for a mud-puddle it seemed....Sometimes we met a black and rusty-looking vessel, laden with lumber, salt from Syracuse, or Genesee flour, and shaped at both ends like a square-toed boot; as if it had two sterns and were fated always to advance backward. On its deck would be a square hut, and a woman seen through the window at her household work, with a little tribe of children....Thus, while the husband smoked his pipe at the helm, and the eldest son rode one of the horses, on went the family, travelling hundreds of miles in their own house, and carrying their fireside with them. Once, we encountered a boat, of rude construction, painted all in gloomy black, and manned by three Indians, who gazed at us in silence and with a singular fixedness of eye. Perhaps these three alone, among the ancient possessors of the land, had attempted to derive benefit from the white man's mighty pockets, and float along the current of his enterprise....

[The countryside passing by] was so tiresome in reality, that we were driven to the most childish expedients for amusement. An English traveller paraded the deck with a rifle in his walking-stick, and waged war on squirrels and woodpeckers, sometimes sending an unsuccessful bullet among flocks of tame ducks and geese, which abound in the dirty water of the canal....Anon, a Virginia schoolmaster, too intent on a pocket Virgil to heed the helmsman's warning—'Bridge! Bridge!'—was saluted by the said bridge on his knowledge-box. I had prostrated myself, like a pagan before his idol, but heard the dull leaden sound of the contact, and fully expected to see the treasures of the poor man's cranium scattered about the deck. However, as there was no harm done, except a large bump on the head, and probably a corresponding dent in the bridge, the rest of us exchanged glances and laughed quietly. Oh, how pitiless are idle people!

Charles Dickens

Charles Dickens rode on the Pennsylvania Main Line Canal from Harrisburg to Pittsburg.

Source: Dickens, Charles, *American Notes* (New York: St. Martin's Press, 1985), pp. 133+.

By the time the meal was over, the rain, which seemed to have worn itself out by coming down so fast, was nearly over too; and it became feasible to go on deck: which was a great relief, notwithstanding its being a very small deck, and being rendered still smaller by the luggage, which was heaped together in the middle under a tarpaulin covering; leaving, on either side, a path so narrow, that it became a science to walk to and fro without tumbling overboard into the canal. It was somewhat embarrassing at first, too, to have to duck nimbly every five minutes whenever the man at the helm cried "Bridge!" and sometimes, when the cry was "Low Bridge," to lie down nearly flat. But custom familiarises one to anything, and there were so many bridges that it took a very short time to get used to this....

Relative to the sleeping arrangements on board this boat....I found suspended, on either side of the cabin, three long tiers of hanging bookshelves....Looking with greater attention at these contrivances...I descried on each shelf a sort of microscopic sheet and blanket; then I began dimly to comprehend that the passengers were the library, and that they were to be arranged edge-wise on these shelves till morning.

I was assisted to this conclusion by seeing some of them gather round the master of the boat at one of the tables, drawing lots with all the anxieties and passions of gamesters depicted in their countenances; while others, with small pieces of cardboard in their hands, were groping among the shelves in search of numbers corresponding with those they had drawn. As soon as any gentleman found his number, he took possession of it by immediately undressing himself and crawling into bed. The rapidity with which an agitated gambler subsided into a snoring slumberer was one of the most singular effects I have ever witnessed. As to the ladies, they were already abed, behind the red curtain, which was carefully drawn and pinned up the centre; though as every cough, sneeze, or whisper, behind this curtain, was perfectly audible before it, we still had a lively consciousness of their society.

The politeness of the person in authority had secured to me a shelf in a nook near this red curtain, in some degree removed from the great body of sleepers: to which place I retired....I found it, on after-measurement, just the width of an ordinary sheet of Bath post letter-paper; and I was at first in some uncertainty as to the best means of getting into it. But the shelf being a bottom one, I finally determined on lying upon the floor, rolling gently in, stopping immediately I touched the mattress, and remaining for the night with that side uppermost, whatever it might be. Luckily, I cam upon my back at exactly the right moment. I was much alarmed, on looking upward, to see, by the shape of his half-yard of sacking (which his weight had bent into an exceedingly tight bag), that there was a very heavy gentleman above me, whom the slender cords seemed quite incapable of holding; and I could not help reflecting upon the grief of my wife and family in the event of his coming down in the night. But, as I could not have got up again without a severe bodily struggle, which might have alarmed the ladies; and as I had nowhere to go to even if I had; I shut my eyes upon the danger, and remained there.

Dickens was lucky; the upper berth held firm....

The washing accommodations were primitive. There was a tin ladle chained to the deck, with which every gentleman who thought it necessary to cleanse himself (many were superior to this weakness) fished the dirty water out of the canal, and poured it into a tin basin, secured in like manner. There was also a jack-towel. And, hanging up before a little looking-glass in the bar, in the immediate vacinity of the bread and cheese and biscuits, were a public comb and hair-brush.

At eight o'clock, the shelves being taken down and put away, and the tables joined together, everybody sat down to the tea, coffee, bread, butter, salmon, shad, liver, steak, potatoes, pickles, ham, chops, black puddings, and sausages, all over again....Dinner was breakfast again, without the tea and coffee, and supper and breakfast were identical....

[T]here was much in this mode of travelling which I heartily enjoyed at the time, and look back upon with great pleasure. Even the running up, bare-necked at five o'clock in the morning, from the tainted cabin to the dirty deck; scooping up the icy water, plunging one's head into it, and drawing it out all fresh and glowing with the cold; was a good thing. The fast, brisk walk upon the towing-path, between that time and breakfast, when every vein and artery seemed to tingle with health; the exquisite beauty of the opening day, when light came gleaming off from everything; the lazy motion of the boat, when one lay idly on the deck, looking through, rather than at, the deep blue sky; the gliding on at night, so noiselessly, past frowning hills, sullen with dark trees...the shining out of the bright stars, undisturbed by noise of wheels or steam, or any other sound than the liquid rippling of the water as the boat went on: all these were pure delights....

We had left Harrisburg on Friday. On Sunday morning we arrived at the foot of the mountain, which is crossed by railroad. There are ten inclined planes; five *as*cending, and five *des*cending; the carriages are dragged up the former, and let slowly down the latter, by means of stationary engines; the comparatively level spaces between being traversed, sometimes by horse, and sometimes by engine power, as the case demands. Occasionally the rails are laid upon the extreme verge of a giddy precipice; and looking from the carriage window, the traveller gazes sheer down, without a stone or scrap of fence between, into the mountain depths below. The journey is very carefully made, however; only two carriages travelling together; and, while proper precautions are taken, is not to be dreaded for its dangers....

On the Monday evening, furnace fires and clanking hammers on the banks of the canal warned us that we approached the termination of this part of our journey. After going through another dreamy place—a long aqueduct across the Alleghany River...being a vast, low, wooden chamber full of water—we emerged upon that ugly confusion of backs of buildings and crazy galleries and stairs which always abuts on water, whether it be river, sea, canal, or ditch; and were at Pittsburg.

The Canals Endure

Some canals endure. The Erie lives as part of the New York State Barge Canal system. Besides freight transportation, canals provide recreation, flood control, irrigation, wildlife habitat, and hydroelectric power. Parks, some with water and some just towpaths along weedy gullies, can be recreational spaces for increasingly urban Americans: hiking, biking, canoeing, and some barging vacations.

Source: Rockland, *op. cit.,* pp. 78-9.

There are landscapes that haunt. It is the archaeological feeling of places where people have been and are no more that haunts. Canals are just such haunting places. They are at that junction between man's works and nature....One reason we tend not to recognize old canals is because they've deteriorated to the point where there isn't much to distinguish them from rivers. Walking along the Delaware and Raritan Canal, one observes its collapsing walls and thick vegetation, the cattails luxuriating in its shallows, the prodigious number of box turtles sunning themselves on its banks; and one thinks: What a quiet, lovely river! But then one comes upon some rusting lock machinery, or a concrete mile marker, nearly engulfed by vines, and realizes that, while nature is fast taking over, evidence of man is still apparent. The ghosts of those who built and used this liquid highway are everywhere.

For those who look.

Suggested Further Reading

The sources cited within the text and especially the following materials are recommended as further reading on America's canal era.

Drago, Harry Sinclair. *Canal Days in America: The History and Romance of Old Towpaths and Waterways.* New York: C. N. Potter, 1972.

Edmonds, Walter D. *Mostly Canallers, Collected Stories.* Boston: Little, Brown and Company, 1934.

——— *Rome Haul.* New York: Grosset & Dunlap, 1929.

Garret, Wilbur. "Waterway that Led to the Constitution." *National Geographic*, vol. 171 #6 (June 1987), pp. 716-753.

Garrity, Richard. *Canal Boatman: My Life on Upstate Waterways.* Syracuse, NY: Syracuse University Press, 1977.

Harlow, Alvin F. *Old Towpaths; the Story of the American Canal Era.* New York and London: D. Appleton and Co., 1926.

Oxlade, Chris. *Canals and Waterways.* (Technology Craft Topics) New York: Franklin Watts 1994 (J).

Rockland, Michael Aaron. *Snowshoeing Through Sewers.* New Brunswick, NJ: Rutgers University Press, 1994.

Scarry, Huck. *Life on a Barge: A Sketchbook.* Englewood Cliffs, NJ: Prentice-Hall, 1982.

Waggoner, Madeline Sadler. *The Long Haul West: The Grand Canal Era (1817-1850).* New York: G. P. Putnam's Sons, 1958.